General Hermann Balck

An Interview

January 1979

Ray Merriam
Editor

MILITARY MONOGRAPH 25
BENNINGTON, VERMONT
2012

First published by the Merriam Press in 1988

Fifth Edition (2012)

Copyright © 2012 by Ray Merriam
Book design by Ray Merriam
Additional material copyright of named contributors.

All rights reserved.
No part of this book may be used or reproduced in any manner whatsoever without written permission, except in the case of brief quotations embodied in critical articles or reviews.

The views expressed are solely those of the author.

ISBN 978-1468188806

This work was designed, produced, and published in
the United States of America by the

Merriam Press
133 Elm Street Suite 3R
Bennington VT 05201

E-mail: ray@merriam-press.com
Web site: merriam-press.com

The Merriam Press publishes new manuscripts on historical subjects, especially military history and with an emphasis on World War II, as well as reprinting previously pubished works, including reports, documents, manuals, articles and other materials on historical topics.

Contents

Chapter 1: Brief Biographical Sketch 7
Chapter 2: Interview with General Balck 11

Publisher's Note

THIS interview was first published in a two very limited edition booklets in 1979.

Chapter 1

Brief Biographical Sketch

Hermann Balck at the height of his career, decorated with the Swords and Oakleaves to the Knight's Cross.

"He was one of our most brilliant leaders of armor; indeed, if Manstein was Germany's greatest strategist during World War II, I think Balck has strong claims to be regarded as our finest field commander."
—Major General F. W. von Mellenthin
Panzer Battles, 1956

BALCK was born on 7 December 1893 in Danziglangfuhr in Prussia. He is the descendant of a Finnish family that mi-grated from Sweden in the year 1120. His father was a Lieu-tenant General with the highest World War I decoration for valor, a noted writer on strategy and tactics, and a member of the Imperial Prussian General Staff.

In the spring of 1913 Balck joined the Goslar Rifles as a ca-det. In February 1914 he was posted to the Hanoverian Military College and in August 1914 he entered combat in World War I with his parent unit.

From 1914 to 1919 he served with his battalion, a mountain infantry unit, as a company officer and company command-er on the Western, Eastern, Italian, and Balkan Fronts. At one period he led a combat patrol behind Russian lines, where it operated for several weeks. During the war he was awarded the Iron Cross, First Class, while still an ensign, and was wounded seven times.

In 1922 he requested transfer to the 18th Cavalry Regiment at Stuttgart, and served with that unit for twelve years. During this time he also had two General Staff tours and twice re-fused invitations to become a General Staff officer. His next assignments were as personnel staff officer of the 3rd Infantry Division and then commander of the newly-established bi-cycle battalion at Tilsit, East Prussia, which was part of the 1st Cavalry Brigade.

Promoted to Lieutenant Colonel in 1938, he was transferred to a post in Guderian's newly-formed Inspectorate of Mobile Troops at the Army High Command in Berlin. This Inspectorate had responsibility for armor, motorized infantry, and cavalry. He was in this assignment at the outbreak of World War II, and during the Polish campaign he oversaw the re-organization and refitting of the panzer divisions.

Then, in October 1939, he was assigned to command the 1st Motorized Infantry Regiment of the 1st Panzer Division in Guderian's Panzer Corps. On 13 May 1940, Balck's regiment forced a crossing of the Meuse River to spearhead Guderian's breakthrough of the French fortifications at Sedan. Mid-May found him temporarily in command of the 1st Panzer Regiment of his division, and he continued in combat until the fall of France at the end of June.

On Balck's suggestion, after Sedan, German tanks and infantry were employed in mixed battle groups, a significant development in the doctrine of armored warfare. Until that time infantry and armored regiments were employed separately.

After the French campaign, he was assigned to command the 3rd Panzer Regiment of the 2nd Panzer Division. In April 1941 his division broke through the Metaxis Line in Greece to oc-cupy Salonika. Placed in command of a panzer battle group, Balck outflanked the British Corps rearguard at the ensuing key battle of Mount Olympus, demonstrating a remarkable capa¬bility to handle armor in seemingly impassable moun-tainous terrain. He had recently been promoted to colonel.

After the Greek campaign he was given command of the 2nd Panzer Brigade for a short time. In July 1941 he became "Economy Commissioner" in the Office of the Director of Army Equipment within the Ministry of War. His job was to make up for Eastern Front losses in vehicles, and during the next four months he stripped 100,000 unnecessary vehicles and their personnel from other unit Tables of Organization and Equipment (TO&E) and provided them to the combat forces.

In November 1941 Balck was appointed Inspector of Mobile Troops (Guderian's position in 1938) at Army High Com-mand, and he visited the Eastern Front to inspect the forces stalled in front of Moscow and reported on their condition to Hitler. He remained in this position until May 1942, when he returned to combat.

He took command of the 11th Panzer Division, participating in battles at Voronezh, the Chir River, Tatsinskaya, and Manichskaya. He pioneered the use of "fire brigade" tactics, in which he moved his division rapidly to a point of penetration, usually by overnight forced march, and destroyed the breakthrough by envelopment or attack on the flank or in the rear. At Tatsinskaya his division encircled and wiped out a Russian tank corps, and in another action defeated a Russian shock army. In January 1943 Balck was promoted to Lieutenant General, awarded Swords to his Knights' Cross, and briefly given command of the Grossdeutschland Division until May 1943.

After home leave, in September 1943 he temporarily re-placed the com¬mander of the 14th Panzer Corps, taking over just before the Salerno landings. During the ensuing inva-sion landings, in which he opposed General Clark's Fifth Army, he was injured in a crash in his command observation plane.

In November 1943, after Balck recovered from his injuries, Field Marshal von Manstein assigned him to command the 48th Panzer Corps in the critical battles at Kiev, Radomyshl, and Tarnopol—battles in which his corps was responsible for the virtual destruction of three Russian armies and the disruption of others.

From 1 August to 20 September 1944 he commanded the 4th Panzer Army. His counterattack in the Baranov area brought the Russian offensive in the great bend of the Vistula to a halt. For this achievement he was awarded the Diamond Clasp to his Knight's Cross by Hitler.

On 21 September 1944 he was appointed Commander-in-Chief of Army Group C in Alsace on the Western Front. There he conducted delaying and defensive operations against the U.S. Third (Patton) and Seventh Armies, and the Free French First Army, in the areas of Metz, Strasbourg, and Belfort, succeeding in his mission to help buy time and conserve resources for the German Ardennes Offensive. In the third week of December 1944 he was relieved of this command by Hitler and reassigned as Commander-in-Chief of the Sixth German Army with two Hungarian armies also under him.

At the end of the war he surrendered his troops in Austria to U.S. XX Corps Commander Major General McBride to avoid their capture by the Russians. He remained in captivity until 1947. During that time, he elected to not contribute to the U.S. Army Historical Division series of interviews and mon-ographs. Balck kept a combat diary from August 1914 to May 1945 which he is now working into a book to be pub-lished in Germany in June 1979 and subsequently in the United States.

SOURCES

Biographical information extracted from von Mellenthin's German Generals of World War II and Panzer Battles.

Chapter 2

Interview with General Balck

Introductory Note

THE following translation attempts to preserve, as accurately as possible, both the detailed content and the style of Gen-eral Balck's conversation. In the interests of clarity, the questions have been consolidated and condensed; General Balck's answers have been translated in their entirety, with the exception of a few anecdotes and some incidental re-marks.

In previous conversations you spoke of the lack of effect of Russian air in the fighting on the Eastern Front. However, you also said that it was better not to drive on the main roads in order to avoid air attack. How do you explain this apparent difference in your assessment of the effects of air?

Let me give you an example. Behind my corps there was a second corps supporting me. At the last moment this corps was taken away, and I was given its two panzer divisions. I ordered the division on the right to make a cross country march to come up to my flank, which the division did quickly and well. The division on the left, which was also supposed to come forward to clean up the left flank, was ordered to move cross country through some wooded terrain and, specifically, to stay off the main road running through its area of responsibility. I forbade the division commander to use this road because on it he might be torn up by Russian air. But this division commander had the bright thought that if he used the road he would be able to advance faster. He did so, and got badly mauled by an air attack.

It's interesting to note, incidentally, that this fellow was a highly rated General Staff officer. Clever, but unfortunately not very practical. So we are always brought back to the fact that cleverness is a curse. Clausewitz once said, "Man needs a harmony of strengths." Unfortunately, our General Staff system caused a great deal of harm by placing one-sided emphasis on cleverness alone.[1]

---

[1] General Balck elsewhere explained that his objection was not to General Staff Corps officers as staff officers with troops but rather with General Staff Corps as an entry way to command.

If air attack mauled this division, wouldn't one have to conclude that Russian air was reasonably effective?

Russian air attacks were occasionally effective, but only when competently executed. In general, Russia is so large, her terrain is so flat, and her roads are so easy to get off that one could always evade or side step an air attack. Overall, the German divisions weren't particularly afraid of the Russian air forces.

Could one say that neither the Russian air nor the German air forces were very important in the outcome of the war on the Eastern Front?

I wouldn't go quite that far. First of all, our Luftwaffe personnel were far better than the Russian personnel. The Luftwaffe was very well led, and its attacks were sharp and well integrated with the ground operations. Throughout the war I experimented with ways to advance the tactical use of air forces.

I'll give you one example. I had a force of Russian tanks that quietly infiltrated into a village to the rear of my corps. In order to get them out, I worked out a combined air-ground attack using both dive bombers and tanks. The attack was so well coordinated that the last bombs fell just as the first tank broke into the village. As a result, the rest of the assault on the village was simple and quick.

You know, the timing was so close in this attack that a bomb fell 5 meters in front of the regimental commander's tank. Naturally, he was not so enthusiastic about air participation.

No one can question that there were individual examples of effective attacks by air forces. However, on average and across the front, would you say that the movement of the troops on either side was seriously inhibited by air attacks?

Even though we occasionally got ourselves into stupid situations, in general we were able to move pretty much wherever we wanted to.

Was this true of the Russians also?

Yes. After all, Russia is so large and flat.

You know, the Russian's main problem is quite different. His difficulty is his own inertia and sluggishness.

On the other hand, the great strength of the Russian is his ability to fall back on primitive methods. A good example of this was in front of Moscow where the Russian Army, although it was in bad shape, took great masses of men, gave each one a mine, threw in a few tanks, and launched them. Even if large masses of them were killed in the process, it didn't much matter to the Russians. In this fashion, they were able to put us, a modern army with the latest equipment, in a hellish position.

I later used the same primitive methods, based on skillful use of mines, against the Americans on the Western Front. As you know, when I took over the Army Group sector from Metz to Belfort, I was given the last dregs: sick troops with stomach trouble, etc. It was useless to use these people at the front. Some I used to man the fortress at Metz, where they held out for about the five days that I had anticipated. After the five days, they fell into the hands of the Americans where they were relatively well off. The rest of my sick troops I converted into mine-laying battalions.

I said to myself, "If I distribute the mines to the regiments, then each regiment will get perhaps 100 to 120 mines, and they will be used only for the regiment's self defense. Operationally, that's insanity." Instead, from Army Group level, I directed the layout of mine fields.

The mine fields consisted of a few real mines and lots of dummy mines. Using the dummy mines, and the otherwise useless troops from the hospital, I was able to keep the whole defense together and to seriously slow down Patton.

It all worked beautifully. After all, when a tank moves out and sees signs of mines, he can't know whether they're fake or real. So he's got to stop and get the mine field cleared, even if it has lots of dummy mines. Of course, the dummies have to have a bit of metal in them in order to ring the mine detectors.

It worked brilliantly. I would never have been able to slow the American attack—and consequently our own Ardennes offensive would never have taken place—if I had not used mines in this way.

Mines are always emplaced in the wrong way. Commanders have a natural tendency to lay them in a thin belt in front of their outposts. That's wrong, because the enemy will simply come up on them and clear them at the first opportunity. The right way to use mines is to lay them in great depth inside your own position—behind your own front screening forces. That way, the enemy's forward troops can't even get at the mines without a substantial effort. You have to make him fight for the outpost positions in front of the mines. After all, that doesn't matter, because eventually you'll have to fight, and it might as well be there as further back.

Anyhow, once you've forced him to work his way slowly into the mine field, you know exactly where his point of main effort is. Then you can eat (envelop) him up with your mobile reserves. With this tactic, I had great success against the Russians at Galicia, as well as against the Americans on the Western Front.

Rivers have to be defended in the same way. Half your forces have to be forward of the river, half behind. If you defend from only one side of the river, the enemy drives up with his equipment, crosses the river where he wants, and then he's on top of you. On the other hand, if you put out defenses forward of the river then he has to clear you away just to get to the river and maybe he can't even reach the place he picked. Thus, you place obstacle after obstacle in his way.[2]

The key thing with mines is to always control their emplacement centrally. If the mines are just given to the troops, every man will put them where it makes him feel secure. And then the enemy will come some other way without ever hitting any of the locally-scattered minefields. The strength of mine warfare is that dummy mines are almost as effective as real ones. If you have only 1,000 mines, you can lay 50,000 fake mines and still get almost as much effect as 50,000 real mines. If the enemy gets bold and decides you're laying nothing but fake mines, you have to make sure he hits a few real ones.

What was the real effect of American air in your experience as commander of an Army Group on the Western Front? Did the American air, which by that time had reached nearly peak strength, really inhibit the movements of your troops?

First of all, you must understand that on the entire Army Group front, which extended from Metz to Belfort, the number of sorties per day usually available to us was zero. In contrast, the Americans typically put up 1,200 sorties per day. In general the results were this: If the weather hindered the American air forces, then we moved freely. If the weather was good, we had to move through woods or wait for night. We had lots of woods in our area, and within these areas could do as we wished, even in daytime.

On the other hand, where the terrain was open, at some critical moments we couldn't move at all—if the weather was clear. After all, the open countryside was being farmed intensively, with ditches, fences, and walls, and so you couldn't get off the roads once you were

---

[2] In a previous conversation General Balck added that if one defends astride a river with beachheads on the far bank, the enemy may choose to attack and cross between the beachheads. If he does, he can then be enveloped from the rear from the beachheads.

found by air. That was very different from Russia, where you could almost always get off the roads quickly to avoid an air attack.

What was your role at Salerno, and can you tell us a little about your experiences there?

At the time of Salerno, I already had my division command experience on the Eastern Front behind me, and I was given my first corps level command in the area around Salerno, including Naples unfortunately. Actually Naples caused me as much trouble as the Americans.

My corps of five divisions was facing General Clark and his Fifth Army. As Clark says in his book, the whole Salerno landing hung by a thread: At the critical moment of the defense against the landings, I crashed in my liaison aircraft, and consequently was laid up for several days.

Under my instructions, the corps scraped together all the assets they had—leaving only a few outposts to hold the defensive positions—in order to have the local force superiority needed for a decisive strike against the Allied beachhead. Unfortunately, the critical but decimated 16th Panzer Division was stopped by two American musical band units that had just had rifles thrust in their hands. This would not have happened if I had been able to command from the point of action.

You know, of course, that General Clark was considering pulling out of the beachhead because things were going so badly for the Allied landing?

Yes, I knew that. We overheard him talking about pulling out on our tactical intercept radios.

What about the influence of American tactical air on the action around Salerno?

There was a tremendous influence of American air on our forces at Salerno. The American air forces were handled brilliantly, and the terrain helped a good deal. The roads were narrow mountain roads, and it was impossible to get off them when under attack.

As long as the American aircraft were still based as far away as Sicily, their response time was too slow and we continued to be able to move and operate on the ground. When the airfields moved in close to the front at Salerno, it became impossible for us to move during the day.

We made two enormous mistakes at Salerno. First of all, Field Marshal Kesselring didn't build airfields near Naples because he didn't want to disturb the local Italian agriculture. As a result, our German aircraft were in storage, and were destroyed on the ground by the American air forces. Secondly, some silly ass on the staff of one of my divisions, without my knowledge, ordered loudspeakers installed at all the strongpoints of the defense. These loudspeakers were intended to order the Americans to surrender as they landed. The American troops might have laughed themselves to death when they heard the loudspeakers but I can imagine no other possible effect.

Later in the war, was American air at Metz as effective as at Salerno? Were you as hindered in movement at Metz as you were at Salerno?

Yes. Movement was perhaps even more difficult at Metz than at Salerno.

What had more effect on your troops and your tactical movements—bombing or strafing?

You must remember that bombing has two effects: a positive effect and a betraying effect. I first learned at Salerno to always have a daily bombing map made up when facing American air. If you saw the bombs falling in a certain pattern, you knew where the next action would occur and could adjust your own forces to counter the move. Later on in France, this betraying effect of bombing continued unchanged. It was more reliable than almost every other form of intelligence concerning the enemy. Clearly what's needed is some skillful way to mask the intentions revealed by bombing.

You can add to bombing information the information given away by journalists who always talked twenty-four hours too early. By listening to their reports, using our tactical intercept radios, we could know exactly what was happening on the American side.

Our tactical intercept radios worked very well. On the Eastern Front, it was as if we were all in the same family with the Russians. The Russians often come apart when dealing with technical matters such as radio security. As far back as the battle of Tannenburg in World War I, where my father was Chief of Field Telegraphy, every day we had the Russian orders well in advance.

Could you tell us some of the aspects of German military tradition that created a particularly fertile ground for the ideas of blitzkrieg and panzer warfare?

That was a development that goes back over hundreds of years. You need to see Prussia's situation in Europe, first of all. Prussia was a small country surrounded by superior forces. Therefore, we had to be more skillful and more swift than our enemies. That started perhaps with Frederick the Great at the Battle of Leuthen where he defeated, and defeated thoroughly, a force of Austrians about twice as big as his own. In addition to being more clever than our opponents, we Prussians also needed to be able to mobilize much more quickly than our enemies.

These ideas were then further developed by Clausewitz and then by Schlieffen. Schlieffen wanted above all to bring home the lessons of the battle of Cannae. My father criticized Schlieffen for one-sided overemphasis on the strategy of envelopment. My father believed that both breakthrough and envelopment had to be equally emphasized. He gave a lecture publicly criticizing Schlieffen for this one-sidedness, and as a consequence was thrown out of the General Staff. Actually, this made him quite happy, because he was a fine leader of troops.

Schlieffen was tremendously important in the development of German military thought, much more so than say von Moltke. He concentrated on means of achieving effective control of the army in battle, which was unbelievably difficult in the era of the mass armies. With the mass armies it was thought to be no longer possible for a commander to lead from the front or from the point of action. Telephony had to be used to control the mass army, and therefore the commander had to attempt to influence the battle from a desk at the rear connected with his troops by telephone.

Actually, to have made real progress in command of units during World War I would have required a completely different organization of communications. Communications would have had to have been subordinated directly to the General Staff instead of having been made a separate branch or inspectorate, as it was in World War I.

The decisive breakthrough into modern military thinking came with Guderian, and it consisted not only of a breakthrough in armor weapons but also a breakthrough in the communications weapon.

As an aside, Guderian was constantly involved in battles with everybody else. He was very hard to get along with, and it's a tribute to the German Army, as well as to Guderian's own remarkable abilities, that he was able to rise as high as he did within the German Army.

His breakthrough in signals was in part, of course, an outcome of his World War I experience as signal officer of the 5th Cavalry Division, which had a very poor division commander. Due to poor leadership, one battalion and Guderian's signal section were completely wiped out in an attack by the French. In his after-action report, Guderian accused his division commander of personal falsification.

Guderian's report went directly to the division commander, and also to my father, who was the division commander's superior. As soon as my father saw the report, he instantly transferred Guderian to be signals officer in the 4th Army.

In any case, Guderian made two very important contributions in the area of panzer warfare communications. The first contribution was to add a fifth man, a radio operator, and a radio to each tank in the tank division. This allowed both small and large tank units to be commanded and maneuvered with a swiftness and flexibility that no other army was able to match. As a result, our tanks were able to defeat tanks that were quite superior in firepower and armor.

Guderian's second contribution was to give the panzer division a signal organization that allowed the division commander to command from any point within the division.

I always commanded my panzer division in the following manner. I always located my Chief of Staff in a headquarters to the rear. I commanded from the front by radio and could thus always be at the most critical point of action. I would transmit my commands to the Chief of Staff, and then it was up to him to make sure that they were passed on to the right units and that the right actions were taken. The result was to give us a fantastic superiority over the divisions facing us.

When Guderian first tried to explain the concept and organization of the panzer division to General Fritsch who was the Chief of the General Staff at that time, Fritsch asked him, "And how do you intend to control this division?", and Guderian answered, "From the front using radio!" Fritsch replied, "Nonsense. The only way to command a division is from a desk at the rear, using telephone."

Wasn't there anybody on the German side in World War I who saw that leading from the rear was a serious mistake?

Yes, Ludendorff recognized the tremendous error of trying to command from the rear, and in fact, in the spring of 1918 he issued a very famous order that was part of the new infiltration tactics of 1918, and this was an order concerning command. He ordered all division commanders in the coming offensives to command from the front lines on horseback. Where this was done, it had a tremendous success. In fact, it had two effects: one tactical and one political. Naturally, the divisions that were led from the front had much greater tactical success than the others. But interestingly enough, those same divisions were the ones that suffered no mutinies during the upheavals of 1918.

This is just another example of the fact that strategy, tactics, and politics all have to work hand in hand. After all, war is never a technical problem only, and if in pursuing technical solutions you neglect the psychological and the political, then the best technical solutions will be worthless.

We certainly agree on the value of commanding from the front; the tremendous effect of a commander who leads from the front has to be seen to be believed.

Sure. In World War II, at Sedan, my combat leaders told me that they were finished—that they just simply couldn't advance anymore, and I said "Fine. Whoever wants to stay here can stay here. I'm leading the attack on the next village," and of course, the entire regiment sprang up as one man to follow me.

What effect did the World War I infiltration tactics have on the development of panzer warfare?

As you know, the machine gun and barbed wire dominated most of World War I and that's why there were no decisive battles except in Russia where there was plenty of room.

Well, this dominance of the defensive weapons was broken just at the end of the war by the tank and the mortar—and that completely overturned the overall tactics of World War I. A tremendous number of our officers in World War II failed because they wanted to continue leading as they had in World War I. The attack had regained an unbelievable advantage over the defense.

There is one more very important chapter that I would like to discuss. When we advanced on Moscow, the general opinion, including my own, was that if we take Moscow the war will be ended. Looking back in the light of my subsequent experience, it now seems clear that it simply would have been the beginning of a new war. The Russians would have switched from modern warfare to the most primitive and ancient means of warfare. After all, they had plenty of room to run all the way back into the vastness of Siberia, and they could have started a partisan war that would have cost us such large forces that our invasion would not have succeeded.

I do not believe that the Russians would start a major technical war against us today. Instead, I believe that they are prepared to wage economic warfare against us, warfare through proxies, and partisan warfare. By these means they will be able to place us in the midst of terrible dilemmas.

I would like to add another matter that I believe is of great importance. And that is the importance of knowing how to use allies. You have to be clear as to what kind of people you are dealing with. Some join you mostly for political convenience and have no other bonds—as for example the Hungarians in World War II. As a result, their divisions couldn't be used in the defense at all, and could only be used to a very small extent in the attack.

Nevertheless, most of our commanders insisted on treating them just as if they were German divisions. As a result of their lack of political motivation, and this poor handling by German commanders, I saw the Hungarian Second Army throw away their rifles and run for home. How do you handle allies like that? We should have never put them together with the Italians and the Romanians in one long unbroken front. A front like that had to fall apart. After all, why should an Italian fight at the River Don? He simply doesn't have any interest in it. No politician can motivate an Italian to fight under circumstances like that.

Instead, we should have split up our allies' forces into smaller groups, perhaps reinforced regiments, and distributed them to German divisions. That might have been reasonably useful, at least for purposes such as rotating German units out of the line for rest and recreation.

I once had the Third Hungarian Army under me. As you know, I didn't think very much of the Hungarian forces. But in any case, to stiffen them I placed individual German battalions in among the Hungarian divisions. At least in the attack that worked reasonably well, until finally the Russians realized that they were facing nothing but a cloud.

I've used that kind of stiffening with weak troops on other occasions. Once I had a German mortar brigade, composed mostly of old men, that was perfectly worthless. But then I gave them five tanks and sent them into the attack, and they worked out beautifully. They had no infantry training, but as soon as the tanks attacked, they ran right along behind. After all, that's all they had to do in order to have a success.

I'd like to return to the question of bombing versus strafing, where you gave us the very interesting answer that bombing could often betray very valuable information to the enemy. How would you compare the actual effect of bombing versus strafing on your troop movements and your trucks?

As you know, to get much effect out of bombing the bomb has to be aimed very accurately, which happens rarely in combat. On the other hand, aircraft machine gun fire makes life extremely uncomfortable on the ground—and seems to leave more margin for error.

It's easy for people to get used to air attack, although it is important to remember that different people react differently to air attack. For instance, the Hungarians and the Italians and the Romanians were never able to stand up to air attack. In contrast, the Russians stand up very well under air attack.

Many people have observed that the Russians—although very tough under some circumstances such as in the defense, under air attack, and so on—sometimes fall apart surprisingly easily. What are your views on whether it's possible to understand the circumstances under which the Russians are likely to shatter?

The Russians, like the Chinese, are very hard to understand. I had quite a bit of experience with the Russians, not only in World War II, but even in World War I when I was commander of a mountain infantry company on the Russian Front and fought behind the Russian lines for a while. In small matters I was able to predict pretty soon what the Russians would do. But in major events I was never able to understand or to predict what the Russians were likely to do, nor do I think that anyone else has ever been able to do so.

The Russians are astonishingly unpredictable and astonishingly hard for a Westerner to understand. They are a kind of herd animal, and if you can once create panic in some portion of the herd it spreads very rapidly and leads to a major collapse. But the things that cause that panic are unknowable. In other things the Russians are hard to predict, too. You may find that for a long time they are mistreating prisoners in an abominable way, and suddenly they turn around and treat them like angels. Some people think that the Russians are likely to collapse when surprised but that has little to do with it. You can't get inside the Russian mentality.

In minor matters some actions of the Russians were predictable if you observed them very closely. For instance, if along the front there was a lot of restlessness at night, and meetings were taking place, and you could hear shouts of "Hurrah!", it was always a sure sign that there would be an attack coming the next morning.

However, during World War II the Russians had relatively few of these idiosyncrasies that gave away their intentions. During World War I, I observed that they were much more likely to indulge in these peculiar behavior characteristics. But as you know, the Russian people changed remarkably between World War I and World War II. By the time of World War II, they really were not the same people at all any more.

Could you tell us something about some of the important changes in armored tactics, formations, and organizations that took place between the beginning of World War II and the end of World War II?

As you know, I developed the basic tactics of the armored infantry when I was in the Mobile Troops Inspectorate. I must say, that in the course of the war the armored infantry tactics didn't change much from these basics, except possibly for some changes in the weapons used on the personnel carriers and technical changes like that. The tactics were essentially the movement and covering fire (Feuerschutz[3]) tactics of the unarmored infantry. You built up covering fire to allow movement forward.

The major difference was that we in the armored infantry used to drive forward as far as possible, using our weapons from the vehicles if necessary, until we ran into anti-tank weapons strong enough to stop the vehicles. At that point we unloaded and proceeded forward on foot just like unarmored infantry. I would say there was very little that changed fundamentally in armored infantry tactics throughout the course of World War II.

Isn't it true that the motorcycle infantry was also a very important component of the blitzkrieg successes, particularly in France?

Most certainly. The motorcycle infantry was particularly important in order to get very, very quickly to the decisive point. The motorcycles were very valuable as a pure means of rapid movement and, as a result, motorcycle units were often far out in front of the tanks. On the other hand, they had some drawbacks. They were very much restricted to paved roads and they were noisy, which made it difficult to do reconnaissance while on the motorcycle.

From the early 1930's, I advocated equipping infantry with bicycles in preference to motorcycles for the reasons that bicycles would be very quiet, would be able to go off the roads onto trails, and would be almost as fast as motorcycles. However, I didn't have the time or the position to fight for this position. I had some actual experience with bicycle infantry because right after the First World War I commanded

---

[3] Literal translation is "fire protection."

a bicycle infantry company, and then later I commanded the first bicycle infantry battalion in Germany. However, bicycle infantry was never very popular with the troops because, of course, all that pumping was more effort than riding comfortably on a nice, powerful motorcycle. Nevertheless, the mobility of the bicycle troops was quite good. It was absolutely no problem to make a hundred kilometers in a day.

Of course, a key problem with bicycles in combat is that they tend to get loaded up with all kinds of stuff that doesn't belong there. The troops are riding along and suddenly they see a goose. "Snap!", the goose's neck is off and she's strapped onto the bicycle. You have a similar problem with tanks, of course. Every tank has its own mascot, and so when a tank unit moves out, it's like a zoological garden going on promenade. Here you have a goat, there you have a hen, and over there you have a goose.

To return to motorcycles, another thing the motorcycles proved to be very useful for was to move out very quickly in advance of the main forces in order to grab a bridge before it could be blown up. This happened time after time in the advance through France, and had a good deal to do with greatly speeding up the rate of movement of our main forces.

What happened later on in the war with motorcycles? Did they disappear due to the mud and heavy opposition on the Russian Front or did they remain a valid means of mobility?

The motorcycle remained useful throughout the rest of the war. And, of course, it remained very popular with the troops because you could carry all those nice things like a goose, a calf, or a bottle of wine on it. The main problem was that the production was not adequate to make up for the losses in the normal combat attrition. And this was what caused the decline of the motorcycle—not at all a decline in combat usefulness.

To understand how this could be, we have to go back to the production situation before the war. In charge of production was my superior, General von Schell, and he was the kind of man who was very willing to accept existing limitations. He would tell you "This is the production capacity we have, more isn't to be had, and you'll have to make do with what you're getting." So, as a result, we entered World War II with peacetime production rates for motorcycles, and they were never increased afterwards. Therefore, as the war went on, and we kept on losing motorcycles to combat attrition and wear and tear, we were never able to replace them adequately. And so the motorcycle units gradually declined in strength.

In the same sense, the crisis of the German Army in front of Moscow at the end of the first autumn was really a production crisis. Because of General von Schell, we were still at peacetime production rates for tanks during that entire autumn. And, as combat attrition accumulated, we wound up with valuable tank crews fighting in black uniforms in the snow as infantry men—and being totally wasted.

General von Schell had extraordinary powers in his position as head of Army Equipment Production in the War Ministry but, despite this, he was never able to control the very powerful automobile industry—because of their political connections. Their interests, of course, were always primarily directed at being in a good position for peacetime automobile production at the end of the war. Therefore, when General von Schell suggested that all the small automobile factories be shut down as a means of increasing the efficiency of production, the big industrialists, of course, were delighted. I made the opposite suggestion—that we strengthen the small factories with some extra workers and use them as our tank depots for the rebuilding and repairing of tanks, because in this way we would get far more responsive tank repair than we were getting from the major companies. Schell and the industry were very opposed to this idea. I was proposed as General von Schell's successor. But I hadn't the slightest desire to take this staff job and I got out of it as quickly as I could.

You know, the Army High Command always used Schell as a means of opposing and inhibiting Guderian. Since our whole General Staff really didn't believe in armored warfare, they were very happy to pit von Schell against Guderian as a way of constraining the growth of the armored forces. Schell himself was useful to them in this regard because he was an extremely ambitious man, and I mean ambitious in a strictly personal sense.

As an example, after the campaign in France, Hitler ordered that the light tanks be re-gunned with the 5-cm instead of the 3.7-cm, and that the heavy tanks get the long-barreled 7.5-cm to replace the short, low velocity 7.5. So Fromm,[4] Schell and I had a meeting to implement this order. Schell announced that it was a requirement that no gun could overhang a tank chassis, supposedly in order to prevent tanks from getting "entangled" in woods. Now Schell had never driven a tank and Fromm had seen tanks only in pictures. And therefore Hit-

---

[4] Minister of War.

ler's order to install long-barreled 7.5-cm guns was not implemented. This was a direct cause of the crisis in front of Moscow. Hitler discovered later that his order had been circumvented and was furious, but Schell was never punished—because Brauchitsch[5] covered for him, having previously illegally directed Schell to hamper Guderian.

The conflict between Schell and Guderian was so bitter that, in order to get anything done, I always had to pretend that the other party opposed it. So I would go to Guderian and I would say "We need to get this done, but Schell is against it," and Guderian would immediately say, "What, Schell is against it! We must have this done." Then I would go to Schell and I would turn the whole thing around and tell him that Guderian was against it, and he would say, "Oh, then we definitely must do it!"

After this happened several times, I went to Guderian and I said, "Look, General, we know each other well; it's time to be frank." Then I explained to him that this conflict between him and Schell was making progress in armored weapons production impossible. Then I explained to him the game I was playing with him and with Schell. Guderian laughed and laughed and laughed, and he said "Fine. You go tell Schell exactly what you just told me, and tell him I'm prepared to resolve our conflict in order to make progress." Well, when I went to Schell, and explained to him the same thing, Schell went right through the ceiling and he said, "No one but you could possibly dare to tell me that." And so we were never able to resolve the conflict between Schell and Guderian, and I went back to playing those silly games.

This incident though, shows you the difference in character between the two men. Guderian was a man of extraordinary character. Later on, when Schell was commander of the 4th Division in my Corps, he failed miserably as division commander in front of Kiev, and I had to report on his performance during these battles. But Guderian sheltered him, took him in, and arranged a job for him at the Armored Warfare School, even though Guderian knew very well how badly Schell had treated him at Headquarters. That's a tribute to Guderian's character.

What was the influence of combat troops on the design, development, and production of tanks and other armored weapons during the war?

In general, not very much influence. Combat troops were occasionally called in and asked how they would address certain problems;

---

[5] Chief of the OKH (Army Headquarters).

but overall, this area was quite heavily dominated by Hitler's direct interest. Fortunately, in determining the technical design priorities among armor protection, mobility, and weaponry, Hitler happened to make exactly the right choice and put the major emphasis on weaponry. But, nevertheless, he was descending from his role as Chief of State to get involved in the muck and infighting of tank development and production. And, as a result of the dictatorship, no teamwork evolved.

The influence of the armored combat troops depended very much on who was Inspector of the Mobile Troops. While I held that position, I did everything in my power to make sure that combat troops would have a great deal of influence. But after I left, not much was done with this position, the troops quickly lost all influence and the office disintegrated.

When I first arrived into this position, I looked over the really filthy situation of armor production and development and decided that the only way to clean it up was to get Hitler directly involved, which I then proceeded to do. That in fact, worked quite well, and I was able to straighten things out for a while.

However, dealing at this level could get you into some very dangerous situations. For instance, in January 1942 I reported to Hitler that the monthly production of tanks was thirty per month and that this was inadequate. Hitler said "No, I just had a report that it's sixty this month"—and I replied, "In that case, you've been lied to." At this point Field Marshal Keitel, who was standing next to Hitler, said "If so, then I am the liar." As you can see, in these situations one was gambling with one's head. You just had to grit your teeth and remain firm in pursuing the greater goal.

Our worst problems in weapons development and production came from the interference of all those lackeys around Hitler and from the influence of the industry. The industry of course, was only interested in what their position at the end of the war would be. As a result, it proved impossible to achieve standardization or a rational choice of vehicles, both armored and unarmored. The situation when I took over command of my division (the 11th Panzer Division) in Russia was so bad with respect to diversity of vehicles that I felt I had to write a very strong letter to Hitler from the front. This letter dealt with the necessity to take over the industry, to get real control over it, and to standardize vehicles and engines in some reasonable way. As it turned out, Hitler never was able to gain control over the industry.

Can you tell us some more about changes in organization in the course of the war?

In 1941-42 I was given full authority to purge excess motor vehicles from TO&Es throughout the entire Army.

What was going on made no sense. One example: it had developed over the course of time that the motorized infantry regiments had collected about ten times as many motorcycles per regiment as their armored infantry counterparts. The infantry defended this, saying that they needed this many motorcycles for command purposes. I replied that, if so, they were providing proof that the infantry is much dumber than armor. In addition to excess vehicles, each infantry regiment had managed to acquire an excess motorcycle infantry company that had no purpose—it was just there for fun.

How do you feel about the idea that the more vehicles you add to an organization—whether it is a regiment or a division—the more that organization tends to clog up the roads and the less mobile the organization becomes?

Of course that is correct. I have always been a strong advocate of small divisions in order to gain maneuverability and mobility. But the most important reason for keeping divisions small is to make it possible for average officers to lead them swiftly and flexibly.

The kind of division organization that I would prefer is about four infantry battalions, half very light and mobile; half armored; one tank regiment with three tank battalions; and one anti-tank gun battalion. That would do nicely and could be easily led.

Such a division would have perhaps ten thousand men—including a separate replacement unit not to be used as a stop-gap infantry unit. Thus, the division would have some ability to regenerate quickly. You know, during the war we never adequately exploited the regeneration capability we already had within our divisions.

What were the changes you observed in reconnaissance units and tactics between the beginning of World War II and the end? I am speaking here of both ordinary reconnaissance units as well as armored reconnaissance units.

Before the war, I helped to reorganize both ordinary reconnaissance units and armored reconnaissance units. In the case of straight infantry divisions, we placed their reconnaissance on horseback and on bicycles in order to save trucks and armored vehicles.

In the cavalry division, the situation was enough to make an old dog howl. They had packed a machine gun and all kinds of accompanying ammunition plus the rider on the poor horse's back. I changed that by introducing load-carrying animals. The horse is quite unsuitable for load carrying, and as an old mountain infantryman from World War I, I had quite a bit of experience with mules. Mules are, of course, incredibly tough. I chose mules in preference to asses, because most of the asses available to us at that time had too few legs—most of them had two legs rather than four. Also, of course, the ass had too short a stride. We bought the mules from the British Army, which was getting rid of their mules. Introducing the mules allowed us to eliminate trucks in mounted cavalry reconnaissance squadrons.

We put the accompanying infantry on motorcycles—thus, no trucks needed. A few armored cars to throw in would have been helpful, but we couldn't get any due to inadequate production.

For the armored units, reconnaissance had to be motorized. Armored cars or light tanks were very important. Later in the war, we were very, very short of armored cars, and I was in favor of using the Russian approach: they improvised their reconnaissance around a couple of ordinary tanks used mostly as vehicles for a decent radio. Thus, they got around having to organize reconnaissance battalions. Of course, it's nice to have specialized reconnaissance units, but only if they are really good and really skilled at their job.

In the 11th Panzer Division I had a superb armored reconnaissance battalion, mostly because it was led by a very, very skillful reconnaissance combat leader, an Austrian who was one of the best soldiers that ever served under me. This officer was able to do phenomenal things with the relatively poor materiel that was available.

Very important is to avoid making reconnaissance equipment heavy. For this reason, we tried throughout the war to develop a decent light tank for the reconnaissance units, but we were never successful. In contrast, the wheeled armored cars worked better, but the eight-wheeler had the serious disadvantage of being much too large and heavy, while the four-wheeler wasn't really mobile enough in cross-country work.

You know, the eight-wheeler was so big and heavy because the reconnaissance troops, naturally, wanted as big a cannon as they could get. Well, that doesn't work. You can't have a big cannon and still have the reconnaissance vehicle light and mobile enough to do good reconnaissance work.

As the war progressed, the infantry divisions simply didn't get any reconnaissance units at all, mostly for lack of equipment—there simply weren't any more light armored vehicles available because they hadn't made the necessary production provisions before the war. Then they were more interested in making cars for family picnics. And of course, the mules were running out, too. So, in general, the infantry divisions had to improvise reconnaissance with captured vehicles, trucks, etc. Trucks were acceptable if you just put in a couple of observers besides the driver. But if you filled up the truck with twenty troops, one hand grenade thrown into the middle of it would wipe out twenty instead of two.

The armored reconnaissance battalions of the tank divisions, in theory, remained unchanged in concept throughout the war: two or three armored cars, a company of motorized infantry, and a company of motorcycle infantry. Actually, they were furnished almost nothing as the war progressed.

Isn't it true that Guderian complained bitterly in 1943 about the fact that the armored divisions on the Eastern Front were seriously neglecting their reconnaissance units?

Sure. I dissolved most of my armored reconnaissance battalions and reduced the rest—simply because the materiel wasn't there. One unit would get the equipment, two would get nothing. So we improvised our reconnaissance from whatever we had available: a few cars or a tank or two. That works too, you know.

In the deep Russian mud of the typical fall or spring on the Eastern Front, was there much difference between tanks of light footprint and tanks of heavy footprint pressure, or between tracks and wheels? Was it possible to see useful, practical differences in mobility between these various vehicle types? Or was it the case that nothing moved in the deep mud, and it didn't really much matter whether you had tracks or wheels?

They all got stuck in the mud.

The real differences were that the ground one division was on might be better than the ground of another division. Then one could move and the other couldn't. Furthermore, there were also skillful and clumsy divisions. One could achieve what the other couldn't. Some divisions became very inventive in bypassing very poor terrain. It was amazing where they could go with just any old truck, if they were clever.

Did you have a chance to try out large divisions alongside small ones to see what their relative effectiveness was?

That experiment arranged itself, frequently. As corps commander, you got both small and large divisions.

Actually, Guderian was a strong advocate of the big division, surprisingly enough. He liked divisions like the Gross Deutschland Division, which I commanded for a while. That division was so big and fat that you could split it in two, and you would have two divisions, each of which would be fat enough by itself.

Now a man like Guderian could lead such a large division. But the average division commander from across the street has to be able to command the organization—that's the real problem. Then clearly the small divisions were superior in maneuverability and speed.

This leads me to bring up an entirely different problem, one that I in fact raised during the war when I was in the Army High Command. I strongly believed that we actually needed three different kinds of armored divisions: one, a heavy breakthrough division; the second, a normal armored division for conducting the usual mobile operations; and the third an anti-breakthrough division for dealing with breakthroughs by the enemy.

The breakthrough division should consist of perhaps two battalions of very heavily-armored tanks with extra-powerful cannons organized into a tank regiment, throw in some light tanks for reconnaissance, and another regiment of two battalions of assault infantry in heavily armored personnel carriers. Unfortunately, we piece-mealed our heavy 45-ton tanks amongst all our divisions, got very little effect from them, and they were mostly quickly lost. For instance, one division got a battalion of forty heavy tanks and the next morning had two left, because they were not technically trained. Instead, we should have gathered the heavy tanks into three or four breakthrough divisions. With these three or four we would have certainly captured Leningrad and, similarly, finished off Stalingrad.

The normal armored division for major operations would be organized as we discussed before.

The anti-breakthrough division was an idea that I had after I had captured about six hundred Russian anti-tank guns outside Kiev. These could have been organized into perhaps two divisions—after being re-bored for German caliber without any noticeable burden on our industry. We could have added a little infantry and some combat engineers. These anti-breakthrough divisions would have been assigned to Army Group level and employed only to cut off enemy breakthroughs—not for ordinary attack or defense. In fact, we constructed one such division, and the Corps to which it was given immediately put it into heavy attack from which it couldn't be extricated. And so the division was wiped out, due to incompetence.

The height of incompetence, though, was the artillery division; a case of clear insanity. In order to compound the insanity, this division—in addition to having an enormous amount of artillery—was given direct-fire cannon battalions that couldn't fight and had no infantry training, and assault gun battalions that were far too immobile. I tried such divisions twice in combat, and they broke down immediately both times. What we should have done was to have organized these divisions into two brigades—perhaps given them a reconnaissance battalion and some combat engineers, and then used them as Army reserves to throw in as support wherever they were directly useful.

What about the usefulness of assault guns?

When Guderian first set up his armor training school many people were opposed and among them, in particular, were the artillerists who were quite angry because they felt that they were the natural home for anti-tank gunnery. So the artillery invented the assault gun to compete with armor.

One of these artillery people became commander of an armored division—and what did he do? He always employed his tanks in batteries of four—and used them as artillery pieces. By this means, he took away from the tanks their greatest strength, which was their mobility. Secondly, the tank crews weren't trained as artillery gunners. Thirdly, the tanks didn't have fragmenting ammunition. After all, when two tanks are shooting at each other, you can stand ten meters away and not get hurt.

So this commander was unable to achieve what he had promised, which was to separate the Russian infantry from their tanks. Instead, what he achieved was a big mess. In its first combat, this division collapsed in no time at all, because it was organized in such a silly way and because the commands it received were so idiotic. When this happened, interestingly enough, the commander was very angry and blamed everyone but himself. This just shows that in the armor business it is easy to have first-class foul-ups.

Did armored reconnaissance tactics change much during World War II?

The tactics really didn't change at all during the war. Only the materiel changed somewhat as we had to start improvising.

The last time that reconnaissance tactics changed in a major way was during World War I, immediately after our first successful attack on France in 1914. At the beginning of World War I, our reconnaissance cavalry was taught to attack recklessly, regardless of the opposition and regardless of the potential losses. They would simply shout "Hurrah!" and ride down whatever opposition they had. The fact that France was in the dark for months after our first major offensive was due entirely to this reconnaissance tactic. We essentially wiped out the French reconnaissance which left them unable to observe and estimate the nature of our first offensive. However, we achieved this at great cost. It cost us the cadre of our best cavalry officers.

Thereafter, reconnaissance tactics changed over to an infiltration type of approach which was used for the rest of World War I and throughout World War II.

Let me add that it is important to understand that reconnaissance is a funny, specialized kind of thing—one man can do it and the other can't—and that is where the biggest differences lie.

What evolution in anti-tank defense did you see during the course of World War II? Was it pretty much the same thing in Russia as in Africa?

Yes, there was little difference throughout the war. What was most needed for anti-tank work was an easily moved, easily handled gun with great penetration—and we needed to have masses of these guns.[6]

The 7.5-cm eventually became the backbone of the anti-tank units and was a good, suitable gun, very similar to the Russian 7.62-cm. The 8.8-cm gun was never part of the normal anti-tank unit organization. The 8.8-cm was found only in flak units. Of course, it was frequently used for anti-tank work by the flak units, but this was a secondary role. And although the 8.8-cm gun had excellent penetration, it was really large, quite immobile, and hard to handle.

We badly needed to assemble decisive concentrations of anti-tank strength by putting together PAK or anti-tank divisions consisting of several hundred guns. These would be used in countering breakthroughs to provide a stiff defense for Soviet attacks to run up against.

---

[6] In a previous conversation General Balck explained the important German concept of panzer divisions being composed of three essential combat arms: tanks, armored infantry, and anti-tank guns (or PAK). The anti-tank guns were not primarily for the defense of the other arms as in U.S. doctrine. Instead, they were to be used to form a strong front to block a breakthrough, or to hold the enemy in place, while the tanks enveloped him or hit him in the flanks or rear.

What was your view of self-propelled anti-tank guns?

I'm somewhat against them. I prefer towed guns because the towing vehicle can become useful then, too, instead of being only a dedicated chassis for the gun. The towing vehicle can be used for transporting ammunition or casualties, etc. If it breaks down, the gun is not immobilized. After all, you can simply take that gun and put it behind another vehicle as a second towed gun.

It is absolutely impossible to get along in armored warfare without anti-tank cannons. Typically, you could start out a battle with fifty tanks and a hundred anti-tank cannons and within a day you might be down to ten tanks but almost all of your anti-tank cannons would still be there. So even though the tanks were quickly lost or attrited, you still had plenty of defensive strength left, and could do something against the opposing Russian forces with your surviving anti-tank cannons.

Also of great importance is good tank repair to turn around broken or damaged tanks as quickly as possible and get them back into battle—and you need this tank repair very near the front. Of course the repair people have a natural tendency to fall back further to the rear—to the nearest spa or resort area. Whenever I took over a new command, the first thing I did was to comb out the most attractive villages and towns to round up these people and get them to work near the front. For instance, when I took over my Army Group, each division's tank workshop was located on the Rhine. And each repaired tank had to make the long climb out of the Rhine Valley, causing most to break down again. Inside twenty-four hours, I had all the workshops practically on the front. You see, good leadership has to take care of these kinds of things.

The troops have to be taken care of—you have to attend to their food, their clothing, their shelter, their medical care—and all these logistics arrangements must function. For this reason, good combat leaders cannot ignore the re-supply and administrative functions. And to really get these functions to operate well, you can do it only from the front—by constantly checking that the troops at the front are actually receiving what the logisticians claim they're providing.

The real nature of combat command is extremely varied: One day you may be dealing with close combat, the next day you will be involved in an artillery duel, and the day after that you have to be commanding economic warfare. You simply have to adapt and use the means at hand.

How did you achieve real cooperation between air forces and ground forces? For example, in the attack on the village in your rear that was occupied by Russian tanks?

The tactical air commander for the Central Front was a very competent, responsible man, General Seidemann. In the battles of my Corps around Kiev, we worked together beautifully. I simply called him in and I said, "Look. We intend to do the following thing about that village in our rear. Do you want to give a hand?" He said "Of course," and from that point on there was no further friction. If the people you are working with are reasonable, you can accomplish everything. If they're silly, you can't get anything done. I didn't concern myself at all with who was to issue the commands, or how many airplanes were to be sent, or any of those details. I simply said, "The panzers are breaking into the village at 5:00, and the last bomb should fall at 5:00. Will that work?" "Yes, it'll work." "Fine, let's go ahead." That was all it took to get the matter accomplished.

But it's not possible that, on the average, your air-ground cooperation could have been this outstanding throughout the entire war. After all, we had tremendous problems in that area, and still do.

You can only solve this air-ground problem in a personal way. You have to put two people together who can work together. This same problem exists throughout all of war. You can't put two people together at a table who aren't able to work together.

Our people were very good at this: putting together two people who were bitter enemies and couldn't work together, and then wondering why things worked out so badly. In this respect, I think the French were well ahead of us. I believe that already in World War I they would never separate a general and his chief of staff if they were working together well. Both would grow together. Our system liked to frequently rotate and change chiefs of staff. You know there's no reason why you can't put a ground general and an air general together in the same way, and allow them to grow together.

Very important in this matter of achieving air and ground cooperation is to not let the bureaucratic aspects stand in the foreground. The only way to solve the problem of cooperation is through the personal relations of the people involved.

Because we got along, it worked beautifully with General Seidemann, and we were able to accomplish anything. If he wanted something from me, I would tell him directly I can do it or I can't do it. Then it would get done or it wouldn't get done. And vice versa, if I wanted something from him. The dominant factor is mutual confidence. I only had one difference of opinion with Seidemann. It happened that I wanted to get some re-supply to one of my units, and I said to Seidemann, "Oh, you can handle that for me, can't you?" And he said, "What! We're attack pilots, not supply troops." And I said, "Okay, okay—the people will get their bread even without you!"

In this matter of air-ground cooperation, you have to give the air an unencumbered area of responsibility—as unencumbered as possible. If you give him the full responsibility to do the job, then you won't be getting a lot of questions on what to do next.

What if you would have had five times as many attack aircraft, and a general as cooperative as General Seidemann to command them? Do you think you would have been able to achieve a great deal more?

I don't think so. I generally achieved whatever I was supposed to achieve.

How were you organized for tank repair? How adequate were your capabilities for tank recovery from the battlefield, particularly during retrograde movement?

At the regimental level we had a maintenance unit for normal day-to-day care of the tanks. At the division level we had a full workshop that could do all kinds of repairs, change motors, etc. For tanks that were too badly shot up and too badly damaged to be repaired at the division, we simply sent them back to depots in the Homeland. We almost never had depots at levels between the division and the Homeland. As far as being able to recover tanks from the battlefield, we had special companies for doing this but we never provided enough capacity in this area. If we had had adequate capacity we would have been able to also recover lots of Russian tanks.

What about using captured Russian tanks?

Even before the war I was asked that same question:

Should we make use of captured Russian tanks or not? My answer at the time was, "Let's capture them first, then we can worry about what to do with them." Actually, there are problems in using captured enemy tanks. The troops generally like to try to use them, but either they quickly get shot up by friendly fire or they get used up very quickly because of lack of spares and lack of crew training.

Then they are wasted and left behind. I have always felt that we should have had a special organization to make use of captured enemy tanks. This organization would recover the tanks, bring them back to depots, fix them up and then find uses for them, preferably in static and defensive positions. At the time, I thought a good use for tanks captured in Russia would have been as dug-in, armored pillboxes in the Atlantic Wall. The important thing, however, is not to try to use them at the front.

Could you give us your views concerning the usefulness of the self-propelled assault gun?

The assault gun was an abortion created by the artillery and our development and procurement organization. As soon as we had created it, the Russians immediately imitated it without any other reason. We found that in combat the assault gun was unusable in armored divisions. The reason was that assault guns were never fast and mobile enough, because of their overloaded chassis. They were somewhat usable in infantry divisions for fire support in infantry assault or defense, or as an anti-tank gun. However, there is no question that a tank would have been far better and much more sensible from a production point of view. The Russians had a fairly good assault gun that was interesting because it was small and quite low. But just as with us, it was certainly not as good as their tank.

Do you feel that artillery in armored divisions should be self-propelled?

In combat, towed artillery was more than mobile enough for armored divisions. If you want artillery to move faster yet, then what you need is a tank, not an artillery piece. I'm convinced that this business of self-propelled guns is more a matter of fashion than of utility. Self-propelled chassis have quite a number of disadvantages including the fact that they are very large and visible and vulnerable to being found by air reconnaissance. Towed artillery, on the other hand, is much smaller, more easily camouflaged, and, of course, you can use the towing truck for many other purposes.

Guderian faced this problem of whether to use self-propelled guns before the invasion into France. He was asked whether he wanted to have self-propelled mortars or the old model of towed mortars for his campaign in France. He said, "Under no circumstances do I want to have anything to do with self-propelled mortars. I much prefer the old model of towed mortar."

We know that speed of response, considering time required to make new decisions and to execute new orders, is essential to fast-moving blitzkrieg operations. How would you compare the relative time to respond of German, Russian, and American divisions in combat? Can you give some specific estimates and specific times?

First of all, you must realize that on many occasions, the Russians did not respond at all, in view of their surprising inertia and sluggishness. I'll give you one example of this: in my corps sector, I ordered an attack on a very narrow front preceded by an artillery preparation using four divisions' worth of artillery. After the attack was launched, we realized that the Russians hadn't paid any attention at all to the preparation.

As a good example of how fast a German division could respond—I was heavily engaged in an attack with the 11th Panzer Division near Chir. Corps headquarters called up at seven o'clock in the evening and said that there had been a serious breakthrough 20 kilometers to my left, and that I should hurry over and take care of the breakthrough. I said, "Well, let me clean up the situation here and then I'll take care of the breakthrough." They said, "No, the situation on your left is terrible, and you've got to seize your attack immediately and clean up the breakthrough as fast as possible." I immediately gave the verbal orders extricating us from the attack and directing the division on how to move and prepare for the new counterattack against the breakthrough 20 kilometers away. We launched our counterattack at five o'clock the next morning, and achieved such surprise that we bagged seventy-five Russian tanks without the loss of a single one of our own. Of course, one of the key reasons why we were able to achieve such quick movement was that I marched with the units. After all, the men were dead-tired and nearly finished. I rode up and down the columns and asked the troops whether they preferred to march or bleed.

To compare our speed with the motions, I would estimate that a Russian armored division would have required at least twenty-four hours longer to have achieved the same movement we achieved in ten hours. I had much less experience against the Americans, so I can only guess that the Americans would have been slightly faster than the Russians.

I have another example where the 11th Panzer Division had just completed a successful attack against some Russians to its front when it got the word that five Russian infantry divisions were directly to its rear. I used fully verbal orders transmitted by radio to turn the division around.[7] We turned around, attacked the five infantry divisions to our rear, and they collapsed in two hours from the time we got the first word that they were advancing on our rear.

The secret of modern armor leadership is that everything has to happen in the blink of an eye. That can only be accomplished if the commander is right at the point of action—and only if the division has confidence that it is being competently led.

This is a question that has very important implications for the feasibility of a successful NATO defense against the Soviets in Central Europe today. We all know that the German Army achieved amazing successes against much larger Russian forces using high speed, mobile defense tactics. However, this was achieved with highly experienced units and leaders. Do you think it is possible for NATO units, with no combat experience and only peacetime training, to be able to apply those same tactics immediately upon the outbreak of a war in Central Europe?

If you have the right people in the right places, I think it may be possible to use mobile defense tactics immediately. If, on the other hand, you have asses as leaders, why then it is impossible.

Can you tell us about the extent of tank crew losses in battles where you took heavy tank losses?

Casualties in the tanks themselves were almost always quite light. However, once the tank crew had to abandon their tank, we often had to employ them immediately as infantry. And at this point we took unheard-of losses among the tank crews because they had no infantry skills.

This is why I feel very strongly that all tank crews as well as all artillerymen and re-supply troops, etc., must have really thorough infantry training before they are put in combat. Very frequently, you have the situation where you simply have to insert those people into infantry combat and, when you do, the losses among them are terrible if they are not trained.

How were your divisions organized to replace combat casualties?

We had a special unit in each division that we called the commander's reserve—consisting of perhaps two to three companies in

---

[7] In a previous conversation, General Balck stated that, as a matter of principle, he issued only verbal orders in combat—and that this was one of the critical elements in achieving real speed of response.

strength—that contained all the trained people that we needed to replace combat losses. This unit might have perhaps twenty artillerymen and forty tank crewmen of different types, etc. We also used this unit as a school for NCOs at the same time.

All this worked well as long as you took extreme care to make sure that nobody under you or above you—at corps level, for instance—used this unit as an infantry outfit to plug sudden gaps or emergencies. Once you permitted that, you could lose all your specialized replacements in a matter of minutes. Eventually, as Army Group commander, I had to retain approval authority for any employment of these division replacement units. You have to remember, every responsible measure will be sabotaged, sooner or later, by front line troops when they feel some urgent need.

Do you agree that units that are too large in combat—for instance, companies of 220 men or divisions of fifteen thousand men—simply incur unnecessary additional casualties without achieving any additional results? After all, there's a limit at every level to how many people a commander can control and the people they control become casualties quickly.

Absolutely. That's why units have to be kept really small. You must keep in mind that you win wars only with men, not masses. The principal of marching masses into combat under little effective control is the principal that the Russians often use.

The Russians clean out the prisons, form companies and battalions, stick a few rifles in the hands of the prisoners and march them off to the attack. They take unbelievable losses—maybe they achieve something and maybe they don't—but in either case the Russians say to themselves "Well, at least we are rid of our criminals."

During your regiment's crucial assault across the Meuse River at the beginning of the French campaign, the Luftwaffe Stukas are said to have played an important role. Could you describe the support they provided you?

Let me retail this action quite briefly. We knew in advance that we had to execute the crossing and I had already rehearsed it on the Moselle with my people. During this practice I had a couple of good ideas. First, every machine gun not occupied in the ground action was employed for air defense. Second, every man in the regiment was trained in the use of rubber boats.

When we got to the Meuse, the engineers [to handle the boats] were supposed to be there. So you see, if I hadn't trained my people, the Meuse crossing would have never happened. Which again leads to the conclusion that the training of the infantryman is reverently too many-sided.

By the way, I had a company of engineers from the Gross Deutschland Regiment at the Meuse crossing. I told them, "Thank God you are here, you can put us across." They said, "We can't, we're assault engineers." I replied, "Assaulting we can do by ourselves—for that we don't need you."

The operation lay under intense French artillery fire. I had thrust forward to the Meuse with one battalion after some brief fights with the French outposts, and I had set up my regimental command post up front there on the Meuse, along with the forward battalion. I went along with them to make sure that some ass wouldn't suddenly decide to stop on the way.

You know, the essence of the forward command idea is for the leader to be present personally at the critical place. Without that presence, it doesn't work. We'll come back to this subject again.

In any case, when we got to the river, the French artillery began to fire and it was a pretty uncomfortable situation. So I sent a message to Guderian asking for a Stuka attack on the enemy artillery. The air attack came quite quickly, in no more than an hour or so.

That wasn't a pre-arranged attack?

No. It was not arranged in advance.

As you know, we had rehearsed the overall river crossing operation in Koblenz.[8] So when we reached the Meuse the only order we got from division was, "Proceed as in the war at Koblenz."

The attacking aircraft went after the French artillery and put it out of action in the blink of an eye. We were very lucky that the French had poor quality divisions at the Meuse. Also, that their camouflage wasn't very good.

We launched the attack across the river at the same time that the Stukas attacked. Another factor helped us greatly: Many of the French troops were drunk and some couldn't even crawl on all fours. In any case, the attack went relatively smoothly. When the regiment had crossed, we were supposed to wait for our tanks to get across. At this point the French armor counterattacked. It was a critical moment, particularly when we noticed that our 3.7-cm anti-tank cannon wouldn't penetrate. My battalions wanted to fall back, but I said "No, you're staying here and the regimental staff will stay here also." So we had to

---

[8] The rehearsal was conducted on the Moselle at Koblenz.

wait to see whether the French or the German tanks would arrive first. Happily, we soon heard motors to our rear and I said, "Here are the German tanks." What did they turn out to be? Two motorized field kitchens!

After a short while, we heard some more rumbling and a platoon of 5-cm anti-tank guns from the Gross Deutschland Regiment arrived. These could, in fact, penetrate the French armor. The first went into position and was shot up by a French tank. The second went into action and promptly knocked off five tanks. With that, the French armor attack ceased. In this situation, you just had to hold on stubbornly.

We pressed on further all that night but eventually the next morning we had to stop and sleep. When we stopped, I had many of the two hundred machine guns in the regiment set up for air defense duties. Soon the French sent in a splendid and very spirited air counterattack. It was just as in earlier wars where the victorious infantry would be counterattacked by cavalry that had been held in reserve. At any rate, the French pilots flew in close formation barely above the ground. It was almost impossible to miss and our machine guns knocked down most of them in flames. We did have some help from one platoon of light flak. It was a real accomplishment and we suffered not one casualty. Afterwards everything was quiet.

Did the French aircraft attack the bridges or your troops?
No, they attacked the troops.

At any rate, I fell asleep and was awakened by my adjutant. He said to me, "Everything has been done in accordance with the order." I asked, "What order?" He said, "The order to thrust forward." I replied, "That's quite a sound order. Who issued it?" My adjutant responded, "Why, you did." I said, "Not a chance." But, in fact, I had issued the order during my sleep.

The attack continued and we ran into a French Spahi brigade. They were the best troops I faced in both wars.

They fought like devils. They had to be dug out of their entrenched positions. The brigade commander and one of the two regimental commanders were killed; the other regimental commander was severely wounded and captured. Only a dozen officers survived; the remainder died.

We pressed on further and reached Bouvellemont.[9] The decisive breakthrough was made at Bouvellemont. My three battalions had moved up to the village and I gave the order to attack. All my commanders said in unison, "We can't do any more. We're finished." I said, "If you can't do it, I'll do it" and I got up to lead the attack on the defended position. All of a sudden they all joined in; not one left me in the lurch. Then we successfully assaulted the position. The French were again completely drunk.

Why was your attack on Bouvellemont the decisive breakthrough?
Because the French had nothing left behind Bouvellemont. Their last reserve was the regiment that had counterattacked us—the one we had stopped by destroying five of their tanks.[10]

Our entire attack beyond the Meuse was made without tanks. We did have three-quarter tracked armored personnel carriers, which were excellent wherever the enemy had no decent anti-tank defenses. I had laid out the equipping of this regiment in accordance with my ideas when I was in the Ministry of War. And surprisingly enough, I had actually been given command of the same regiment. After all, the personnel office didn't always assign people where they belonged. You know, Guderian was given a reserve infantry corps for the Polish campaign. Of course, he raised a terrible commotion and the assignment was changed. Our personnel office was not our greatest strength.

Was your entire regiment motorized and mounted in armored personnel carriers?
All three battalions were motorized and all the regiment's riflemen were under armor.

If you're interested, we can continue with some observations on the effects of air. Dunkirk brought out some clear lessons. I pushed forward close to Dunkirk. There we underwent some spirited attacks by British pilots. But they didn't really hold us up.

And at Dunkirk our leadership made an enormous error. As you know, the troops were held up and were told that the Luftwaffe would take care of the rest. But, in fact, the air was in no position to accomplish such a task. We had drawn false conclusions from the air attacks

---

[9] Bouvellemont is about 20 km southwest of Sedan.
[10] Balck's real stroke was that he so aggressively pressed forward all night after successfully crossing the Meuse, instead of stopping to rest and consolidate his bridgehead.

in Spain and Sedan.[11] The British did leave behind their equipment at Dunkirk, but they successfully rescued their men. And with these men they won the Africa campaign. If we had simply pushed forward on the ground, all these men would have ended up in captivity.

Did you have any problems with German air support bombing German troops?

Yes. At the Sedan breakthrough. Just after we had beaten off the last French tank counterattack, all our regimental commanders were called together to receive orders at a fork in the road. The Luftwaffe attacked right at this point and those present were wiped out. An armored brigade commander and two regimental commanders were killed. At the time this happened, I was still on the way to the meeting.

Was there any means of radio communication between attack aircraft and the motorized ground units at that time?

No. That came later.

Were there any changes in air support procedures or other consequences of this incident at Sedan?

The only consequence I know of is that I had to take over an armored brigade.

There was no change in air-ground liaison procedures because that sort of thing doesn't happen so fast. To get there lots of people have to change their thinking—most of them people who don't want to think at all. Many wish to avoid drawing any conclusions at all; they find it easier to say that an accident like that is a unique occurrence.

Later, in the Greek campaign where I had a panzer regiment, there was essentially no air-ground cooperation. I saw only one Stuka attack. The English air force attacked us courageously and well, but only for the first few days. After that, they disappeared to Crete.

Why didn't the Stukas provide you with more help?

Oh, we didn't really need them much. It went very well without them.

But I am convinced that the English could have completely stopped the German conquest of Greece if they had properly employed their air. The roads were narrow mountain roads filled to over-

---

[11] The air attack in support of the Meuse crossing.

flowing with our columns. By hitting us at the right points they could have caused us boundless losses.

One of the narrowest and toughest spots to get through was the Tempi Gorge.[12] At this point I had a mixed battle group, one panzer regiment plus an infantry battalion, an artillery battalion and a motorcycle infantry battalion. But I only pushed through the gorge with one tank company and one armored infantry company. Everything else I left outside the gorge because of the threat of artillery coverage down the length of the gorge. After all, the effects of artillery are increased tenfold in rocky mountainous terrain because of the stone fragments. If one went in there with lots of people, the losses would be very high. I went in with only a few and had almost no losses. To get through, I had to dress up my tanks for water crossing and I put them across the river like submarines. The British thought it couldn't be done and were astounded when I appeared at the other end of the gorge.

How did you use your motorcycle infantry battalion in this action?

As soon as they arrived, I took away their motorcycles and used them as mountain troops against the New Zealanders' positions in the hills. After all, I'm an old mountain infantryman myself. I told them, "Don't cross this line. You can cry as much as you like but take the long way around and come from the rear." Just before launching them, I mounted a feint frontal attack with some tanks. Then I brought the motorcycle infantry down into the rear of the New Zealanders and their resistance fell apart.

Do you know when the concept of the mixed battle group (Kampfgruppe) was developed?

During the French campaign. The originally developed tactic—that is, that the tanks attack and the infantry follows to conduct secondary operations or to roll up something—this tactic was already abandoned by the end of the Polish campaign. The idea of separate assignments for tanks and infantry was a sin against the essence of tactics: the cooperative employment of all arms against a single point rather than using one arm here and another over there.

---

[12] This is a deep, rocky river gorge of some 20 kilometers length running through the foothills of Mount Olympus. For an account of this action based on Balck's regimental reports at the time, see pages 41-44 of *Panzer Battles* by F. W. von Mellenthin, University of Oklahoma, 1956, and Ballantine Books, 1978.

When were the first battlegroups formed—after Sedan?

Yes. That happened quite automatically. When I took over the panzer brigade, it had one armored regiment, two infantry battalions and some artillery. In essence, there was the battlegroup, fully formed. That was the great advantage of the original Guderian organization of the armored division: You could use it to continually form battlegroups to suit the need—here a strong one, there a weak one.

What was the difference between an armored brigade and an armored regiment?

At that time, our organization still had an armored brigade with two armored regiments. That was the success of the battlegroup, that you needed only one armored regiment if you employed all the other necessary arms together in the battlegroup.

Thus, when I took over my brigade after Sedan, the second armored regiment had already been given to another battlegroup. My old infantry regiment was similarly split: My new brigade had one of its battalions; the remaining two infantry battalions were with the other battlegroup.

When you were Sixth Army commander in Hungary and Rumania, the Germans apparently were quite strong in armor divisions but weak in infantry. As a result, you could win brilliant tactical victories through maneuver almost every day, but you couldn't retain the terrain. Would you comment on the question of balance between armor and infantry?

Oh, I think the balance of the peacetime forces was good enough. All we needed to do was to keep them up to strength in war, that was the only little problem!

Did you have this problem of balance in Russia?

The Russian is a unique type. You can risk things with the Russians that you couldn't risk with any other power in the world.

At Budapest, I attacked forty-five Russian divisions with about seven to nine of my divisions. It worked pretty well. If I had had two more armored divisions, I could have cleaned up the whole Budapest area. But Hitler could never make up his mind to weaken a sector in order to have overwhelming strength at a decisive point.

The Russian is passive and slow-moving, terribly slow-moving. You have to get inside the Russian psychology. Then you come to very different conclusions, including tactical ones. When facing the Russian you can't sit down and calculate that he has so and so many divisions or weapons or what not. That's all baloney. You have to attack him instantly and throw him out of his position. He is no match for that.

To discuss the Russian approach, we have to look at not only the last war but earlier wars. We can start with Charles XII of Sweden. He defeated the Russians at Narva, defeated them everywhere. What did the Russians do? They built up an army and trained their commanders and troops in serious warfare. Finally, they reached the point where they were a match for the Swedes. They could afford the time to do this because they had boundless men and because they could withdraw as far as they wanted to. No one ever reached Moscow without paying a price.

In the Second World War, it was much the same thing. The Russians were unbelievably sluggish and incompetent to employ their overwhelming masses.

Here's how it was at the Chir River in front of Stalingrad where I had the 11th Panzer Division. The Russians had their Fifth Tank Army under Koniev. Koniev would launch a tank corps to attempt a breakthrough. He would give the orders on the spot and then move on. So the attack would go in. Naturally, it cut through our thin defenses like a knife through butter. Then the attack would stop; the Russians didn't know what to do next. You had to wait for this moment and then counterattack them immediately. In the blink of an eye they'd be destroyed. In the meanwhile, Koniev would have moved on to the next corps. Same game all over. Attack, etc. Then they in turn would get wiped out.

In this fashion, with one division I eventually broke up the whole Fifth Tank Army. It was possible to do this only because the Russians hadn't trained their commanders yet. Then in the next year their commanders improved.

They were better selected and received more training and experience. That made things much more difficult for us.

On the Chir you had relatively more infantry than later in Hungary?

Not at all. We had far less infantry on the Chir than in Hungary. The people who fought as infantrymen on the Chir were bakers, store keepers, etc. On that whole long Chir front we had almost no artillery. In such a situation, one must not be misled into tying down a division along such a long front. Instead, one must remain completely mobile and attack wherever it's necessary.

What about reorganizing units after heavy losses?

You know, in World War I we already had the so-called commander's reserve. Each unit down to battalion and company level organized such a reserve for itself. For instance, in my Jäger Regiment 10, we established a commander's reserve for the concluding battles of the war. I belonged to this unit because our commander wanted me held in reserve as his replacement in case he fell. I then selected and held in reserve five or six of the best people in my company. None of us was allowed to join in. As a result, when the fighting was over and the Alpenkorps[13] was pulled out, we had enough leaders left to organize around. So we received a few replacements and in the blink of an eye we were in sound shape.

It's less a question of the number of people available and more one of having a reasonable organization.

Were you prevented by higher headquarters from extensive reorganizations after heavy losses? Did Hitler refuse to let the German Army eliminate headquarters or major commands, even after they had no assets left?

Yes. He had this idiotic idea—he wanted to use these many headquarters for deception. In war you can deceive once, but you can't keep on deceiving with the same ruse—that will always miss its mark.

Hitler was continually setting up new divisions, in order to show how strong he was. These new divisions, even when they were stuffed full of people, were worthless.

Did division commanders have the freedom to reorganize as they wished?

I always reorganized as I pleased. Other division commanders, if they were sound, did the same. Those who didn't were types who were likely to founder—if not because of poor organization, then for some other reason.

As a division takes heavy losses, do you think it should temporarily reorganize, for example, from three regiments down to two?

There's a certain weakness in that approach. I would leave the regiments unchanged as long as possible. It's quite all right to occasionally let a regimental commander stand and fight somewhere with fifty men. The troops do more because of *esprit de corps*, because they sentimentalize their own regiment. If they get stuck in another regiment, they

---

[13] A mountain infantry corps that Balck's regiment belonged to.

don't achieve anything. Instead, they keep on saying, "In our old outfit, it was all much nicer."

So does that mean that, instead, the regiments should temporarily consolidate their battalions and companies after heavy losses?

Normally, our regimental commanders would leave the companies alone. Often, the companies would be down to one leader and eleven men. That was better than introducing lots of strangers into the company.

After all, combat leadership is largely a matter of psychology. As much as possible, I tried not to tell my people what to do. As long as I saw that a man was sound, I let him do things his way, even if I would have done them differently.

What about staffs? Didn't you need to cut them down as the units shrank?

By and large, the idea of pulling out excess staff occurred quite naturally. Our people weren't bashful in this regard.

What about combing out the rear area people to get replacements for the front line?

I didn't do it. I generally left it alone because the "hero" of the communications zone is rarely a front line hero. I much prefer one man who fights than ten who look over the situation and then pull out.

But I am firmly convinced that all rear area people need to receive thorough infantry training before they are sent out. It can't be done in the war zone. And every rear area column commander needs to be capable of leading his people in a fight.

I remember, as division commander, going to visit some of my rear area units to thank them for a job well done. While there I decided to test them with a few simple combat problems such as taking a house or holding a village perimeter. The results were shocking: People who could do their maintenance or supply tasks perfectly in the midst of the heaviest bombing or artillery attacks failed miserably. They just didn't know anything because they weren't trained.

Every rear area column needs to have some light anti-aircraft and some light anti-tank weapons. As army commander in Poland, I ordered all the rear area units to organize and train tank-hunting detachments armed just with the "Panzerfaust." Shortly thereafter, the newly-formed detachments from one corps' rear area destroyed seventy-two Russian tanks in a day.

Did you find that the advent of the "Panzerfaust," which I believe was the first really effective shoulder-fired anti-tank weapon in the war, made a big difference to your infantry?

It was a big step forward, but the troops had to be well trained with it first.

You know, initially the troops are always against every new piece of equipment. "Aw, it causes more work. It has to be carried. We did fine without it." The next thing that happens, the new weapon is packed away with great care—just where it can't be grabbed when needed.

The tendency of troops to stick to what they're trained for is remarkable. For instance, in the Greek campaign I and my regimental staff ran into a retreating Greek column. They were clearly getting ready to fight. I had with me only the regimental clerk with a submachine gun. I told him "Stand here, keep a good lookout and shoot if anyone tries to come through here." "But colonel, I have no submachine gun training." I don't know whether he thought I was going to stand there and do it myself. I roared at him till he thought I was the devil himself and then we got on with it.

Another example is from World War I. In those days no light infantryman was trained to throw grenades. Instead, I remember how every evening an engineer with two grenades would report for duty at our position. We'd give him a swig of schnapps, tell him what a great job he was doing, and stick him in the furthest forward foxhole. Then if nothing happened during the night, he'd leave in the morning and report again the next evening for grenade duty.

With this experience of troops pursuing only one skill, as soon as I became commanding general of a division I went to inspect my artillery's abilities. I found not one battery that could serve its machine guns. They were all very carefully packed and put away. So my artillery was given a little extra training.

These are all psychological matters; organizing units has to be done by a man who understands troops and who knows what works and what doesn't. Fundamentally, all troops are lazy—which you can't hold against them. They get run around the countryside enough so that they say, "Here's a little quiet, thank God—don't tell us about anything, we just want to sleep a little." It's understandable, but it doesn't help.

When the troops got enough training, the "Panzerfaust" worked well?

It worked brilliantly. There were people who were really sharp with this weapon. It took a while, but eventually the troops had real confidence in the "Panzerfaust."

Of course, there were always people who would let a tank roll over them. When the tank passed, they would jump up and clap a magnetic mine on the back—gone was another tank. They were fantastic soldiers.

It has appeared to some that the Eisenhower-Bradley emphasis on phase lines, unit boundaries and "line abreast" advances—perhaps intended primarily to keep any one ally from getting out ahead of another—suppressed a good deal of the natural American inventiveness and aggressiveness. As commander of an army group on the Western Front, what was your experience in facing American units?

Within my zone, the Americans never once exploited a success. Often Von Mellenthin, my chief of staff, and I would stand in front of the map and say, "Patton is helping us; he failed to exploit another success."[14]

In fighting the Americans, did you notice the practice of American higher commanders to halt their units at night? Presumably this also meant that these units had to break through a new defensive "crust" every morning at a considerable cost in casualties.

Certainly. It was a blessing. It gave us all night to build new defenses.

Mistakes like these only underline the absolute need for command from the front in modern warfare.

What was your view of night assaults as distinguished from movement or infiltration at night?

I avoided night assaults, mostly because our people weren't capable of carrying them off. In fact, on the Russian front we fought more at night during World War I than during World War II.

What about attacking in tanks at night?

If possible, don't. Our armor people were very much against fighting at night because they could see so little from their vehicles.

---

[14] Balck was commander of Army Group G at this time, from 21 September to 22 December 1944. During most of this period Patton was under orders not to make a major advance.

Does infantry have a great natural advantage over tanks at night, since they can see better than tanks and can hear the tanks from a great distance?

Certainly. That is why my tank commanders refused to attack at night in the Tempi Gorge engagement. They knew they were likely to suffer murderous losses.

How did you control the inevitable tendency of headquarters staffs to grow and grow?

The most important thing was that I gave all orders verbally. Even my largest and most important operations orders were verbal. After all there wasn't any need for written orders. As division commander, I forbade the use of written orders within my division.

To lay on a division attack, I preferred to meet my regimental commanders where we could look over the critical sector and have a terrain discussion. At the end of the discussion, I would tell them, "All right, now we'll do thus and such." Those would be my verbal orders for the attack and that was the end of it.

I always prized most highly those commanders that needed to be given the least orders—those you could discuss the matter with for five minutes and then not worry about them for the next eight days. Manteuffel, who served for quite a while as a division commander in my corps, was one of this type.

About how big was your armored division staff?

Including staff officers, non-commissioned officers, drivers, radio operators, clerks, etc.—it was about fifty people. The less there were, the less aggravation.

When I took over Army Group G, the traffic discipline was in terrible shape so I called in the head of the military police for the Army Group. You know what he told me?

"I'm only the commander of this unit. I have no staff position so I can't be held responsible."[15] He was on his way home the next day.

The staff of Army Group G was about three hundred to four hundred people, again including all the drivers, radio operators, etc. The staff at army level was about the same size while at corps level it was about half that size.

---

[15] It is believed that Balck was referring here to his refusal to have service units commanded via an extra layer of service chiefs on his staff—a system that requires two levels of staffing—rather than the unit staff performing both roles.

If your predecessor commanding one of these staffs was a bit neglectful, then you could have a major housecleaning on your hands. However, I rarely found it necessary to get rid of many people. You could pull just one or two ears and get the same effect because, first, word travels like lightning inside a headquarters staff and second, after one or two of these house-cleanings, I had such a terrifying reputation that my reputation alone would have the needed effect.

I also made it a matter of principle to insist on a small table for supper. I ate only with my chief of staff and any newly-assigned officer going to the front or any unit commander coming back from the front. The staff hated this arrangement but, of course, the information I obtained from these officers going to or from the front was invaluable and couldn't be heard anywhere else.

You probably know that Seebohm's radio intercept company under Rommel in North Africa has become quite famous as a result of the African campaign histories. Did your radio intercept units in Russia and on the Western Front work equally well?

We obtained excellent radio intercept information from the Russians—and equally good information from the Allies. On the Western Front we could get almost no Luftwaffe reconnaissance intelligence, so we were quite dependent on our radio intercept units—they were able to keep us very well oriented.

How would you compare Model's leadership approach with von Manstein's or von Manteuffel's?

Do you know that I had a meeting with Model where I asked him to change because his command techniques were wrong? Of course, he was a very energetic man and had some notable successes. However, his approach was mainly to pump up people to stand fast and to build fortifications wherever he thought someone might attack. His position defense approach was completely opposed to my views on mobile defense. If I have six armored infantry battalions, I won't stick them into the defensive line. I'll hold them in reserve and, when the enemy attacks, I'll use my mobile reserves to throw him out.

I had a terrible row with Model. I told him, "It won't work your way. The troops are good. They've always performed as they were supposed to and will continue to do so. But if you constantly push them and shake them up, their nerves will really fail them." The most serious thing was that Model was always contradicting himself. Today he told his troops this was right; tomorrow the opposite. He lacked the calmness and steadiness that the troops need.

Model listened to everything I said. We both expressed our opinions, shook hands and returned home. He never came to see me again. But every time I got a new assignment, he was one of the first to congratulate me.

That was one of the great Prussian military traditions: you expressed yourself bluntly but you were expected to never resent such blunt criticism.[16]

What was your view of the tactical importance of smoke?

I'd like to describe briefly for you a fight in the northern Caucasus area. One of our armies, the Seventh I believe, was pushed back by the Russians and the Russians crossed the Manitsch River. Our army had no luck in trying to throw the Russians back across the river. My division was ordered to clean up this situation.

We first attacked across the river to try to put the whole Russian bridgehead in a sack. It didn't work. So then I withdrew my troops and attacked the bridgehead frontally where the Russians had dug in all their tanks. When the Russians noticed this second attack, they were naturally very pleased that I was attacking their strong point. I halted the attack so that they wouldn't realize what I was doing. Of course, the Russians were even more pleased to have successfully blunted this second attack.

At the same time, I laid smoke shells on the first positions I had attacked—and drove up lots of trucks in the midst of the fog. Simultaneously, I smoked the dug-in tank strongpoint and unexpectedly broke in there using my tanks and one motorcycle infantry battalion. The Russian corps in the bridgehead was completely destroyed. We lost one dead and fourteen wounded; the Russians had terrible losses.

It's quite remarkable that most people believe that the attack costs more casualties. Don't even think about it; the attack is the least costly operation.

I first saw that clearly in 1914. We attacked an English hill position in northern France. We approached to about 300 meters. The English were just reinforcing to launch some counterattacks as a cover for major withdrawals. The commander of our company in the center said, "If the English reinforce, we're lost—so we've got to get up the hill before the reinforcements arrive." We blew our signals and launched

---

[16] Balck was Model's subordinate at the time of the incident he describes.

the attack. The result was that the English were overrun and thrown out, and the losses were as follows: our light infantry battalion of 310 men buried thirty; the English buried 250 men and lost 250 as prisoners. And from the heights we could see the English army in retreat. For an attack under most unfavorable circumstances, these results are typical relative losses for the attack and the defense.

The matter is, after all, mainly psychological. In the attack, there are only three or four men in the division who carry the attack; all the others just follow behind. In the defense, every man must hold his position alone. He doesn't see his neighbors; he just sees whether something is advancing towards him. He's often not equal to the task. That's why he's easily uprooted. Nothing incurs higher casualties than an unsuccessful defense.

Therefore, attack wherever it is possible. The attack has one disadvantage: all troops and staffs are in movement and have to jump. That's quite tiring. In the defense you can pick a foxhole and catch some sleep.

Did the armored personnel carrier really provide a major advantage over trucks for carrying infantry?

Yes. The advantage was tremendous—above all else, because it pumped up the morale of the troops so much. It also had its disadvantages: If the leaders were foolish, they would fill a whole carrier with troops just to go reconnoiter. It was witless. The first thing I did as regimental commander was to forbid such nonsense. After all, it was adequate for reconnaissance if two men sat in the carrier. The rest were better off staying home.

Today's armored personnel carriers are quite different insofar as they are now closed on top, allegedly to protect against artillery air bursts. What's your opinion of the closed-in personnel carrier?

Low. When the carrier is forced to stop to change over from armored attack to foot-mounted attack, you must be able to jump out immediately. If you are sitting enclosed in armor and have to exit through a door there'll always be a few left inside.

I am against the closed box. What's needed are only armored sides high enough that a man can duck behind them. If this thing runs over a mine, the men inside the closed-in box will be dead.

What measures did you take to secure your headquarters—to protect against ground or air attack?

None. You have to address this problem differently. First you have to understand how the enemy operates. The Russians did as follows. They would attack on a given front. We had a tendency to place our headquarters at a major road intersection behind the center of the front.

The Russians would grab for the intersection and the headquarters and, first thing, we'd lose our command.

I always placed my headquarters differently: in the middle of a woods, off to one side, etc. Then I distributed my command radios over a wide area and tied them together with a telephone net—so I couldn't be located by radio direction finders.

Above all else, I always tried to pull back my headquarters well before any troop withdrawal, because it is essential for the commander to be reachable during a withdrawal. If you have to intervene personally up front, nowadays you can always get forward quickly. In contrast, most commanders kept their headquarters forward and then, at the decisive moment, lost their staffs, their communications, and the command of their troops.

It's terribly important to keep the troops under very tight command during withdrawals. But you can do that only if your headquarters is not in motion and is sitting securely to the rear. Here prestige doesn't matter. Most commanders become very involved in such a situation and say, "I'll stay near the troops," but that's wrong in this case. I'm all for forward command, but everything has its limits.

The skill in selecting a headquarters site is this: to select a place such that, when the Russians make a large-scale enveloping attack, your headquarters is sitting well back and you can calmly take the necessary decisions.

Were any of your headquarters ever hit by air attack, either in Russia or on the Western Front?

In Russia, I almost got hit once. I had my corps headquarters near a village. I stepped out of my door one morning, looked around, and said, "You people are out of your minds." Someone had just established an airfield for medical evacuation right next to my headquarters! I said, "This won't take long before it's seen. Move the headquarters immediately." We had just finished moving when the whole village was razed.

In the West, my army group headquarters was first near Strasbourg. But I soon moved because, after every air attack on Strasbourg, my communications wires would be cut. The next location was further north near the old Reich boundary. Although the Allies were constantly searching for that headquarters, they never found it because I scattered my radios so widely.

I experienced the opposite once when a newly organized SS division was assigned to my corps in the fighting near Tarnopol. Of course, this division made every mistake it was possible to make. First of all, they established their headquarters on a main road and concentrated everything they had in that village—all their radio transmitters and everything. At night I went to see them. During that night 160 bombers attacked us. But it happened only because the radios were right there. The result was that all their communications were destroyed—all due to the incompetence of the responsible commander. A headquarters has to be scattered so that it can't be found. If one transmitter is found, it has to take a long time to find the next.

In our last conversation, you mentioned an Austrian officer who you said was one of the finest soldiers and best reconnaissance leaders who ever served under you. Could you describe some of the characteristics and tactical ideas that made him so good?

Yes. That was Baron von Hauser. He was commander of my 11th Panzer Division motorcycle infantry battalion, not my armored reconnaissance battalion. As you know, I dissolved most of my armored reconnaissance units for lack of recon vehicles.

First of all, he really understood how to take care of his people. Time after time at critical moments, I found they had just eaten. To counter the Russian cold, he took some trucks, installed a little oven in each, and placed them just behind his front. All his troops were rotated periodically to spend a couple of hours warming themselves next to the oven. In the Siberian cold, you have no idea how useful that was.

Next, he had some good ideas for defending against tank attacks. For instance, the danger in a tank attack is that, if you have a long trench line, the tank will place himself over the trench and will fire down the length of your trench. Hauser laid out his trenches in short, irregular zigs and zags. When the Russian tank arrived, our infantrymen could use the cover of the winding trench to get close enough to use magnetic mines or demolitions.

He was a very tough customer and came from an old line of soldiers. When we pulled out of the very heavy battles in the Solzhinitzye Bend, every man in his battalion was in fine fettle while all the other troops had their ears drooping.

Hauser commanded his motorcycle troops in a highly mobile, nimble way. I remember he was defending a very long front. The Russian attacked heavily and Hauser drove quickly around into his rear with his motorcycles and rolled him up.

In general, the motorcycle battalion was most useful as a very mobile reserve, to attack where it was most necessary or to block an important approach route.

What did the motorcycle infantry have for anti-tank weapons?

I often gave them anti-tank guns from my anti-tank battalion. They also had anti-tank grenades and mines and could handle tanks by themselves. It was a brilliant battalion, due to their commander's spirit.

Can you comment some more on the tactical use of smoke?

When you use smoke, the enemy doesn't know whether you're really coming or not—that's the great strength of smoke. But you have to be very careful not to betray your plans through the use of such means. Otherwise, the enemy will know you're coming. When I used smoke, I always applied some where I didn't intend to attack and thereby pulled the enemy into the position where I wanted him.

On the other hand, I experienced a number of smoke attacks in World War I. One large smoke attack was launched against us by the Italians. When they arrived through the smoke, we only said, "Lay your guns over here, then please march in that direction."

What did you do to control the natural tendency of units to exaggerate reports of enemy losses?

I always checked directly on these reports. I would arrive on the spot and say "All right, show me where the eleven hundred dead are lying. And we'll do some counting." It would turn out to be maybe fifty.

But much more difficult and much more serious is the matter of reporting for the distribution of fuel.

At one time, I had just gotten a new divisional chief of staff. He came to my commanders' meeting and complained that all fuel reports were being falsified. I interrupted and said "Please be quiet. When the tank regiment reports that they have absolutely no gas and can't move, I know that they have precisely three combat hours and 50 kilometers of movement left. When the engineer battalion reports that they have no gas left, I know they mean just that.

"It took us a lot of effort to calculate this table of correction factors—please don't mess it up. Just keep on working the way we have been doing it up to now. We know exactly who's lying and who's not and we use that to divide up our fuel."

You know, you have the same problem [of casualty reporting] with tank kills. For instance, three anti-tank guns shoot at a tank and knock him out—each gun reports a kill. Back to the rear comes a report of three tanks knocked out. If you add all those kinds of reports together ... You have to say, "Where are all these shot-up tanks? I'd like to count them."

To deal with such matters first of all you must understand troops. Secondly, you must be able to get some fun out of these problems. They can only be solved with a touch of humor.

Of course, in a way it's a problem when the troops hide what they have. But it's their ingenuity at finding one more gallon and one more round that often saves the day. Did you find the same problem when your troops were reporting on their ammunition situation?

Oh, sure after all, you get to know these guys. If you know your people, then you'll know exactly that this one is lying by fifty percent, that one is not lying at all, and this one over here is understating. You can only figure these things out if you work closely with the troops. Therefore, keep on going forward to see them, listen to them, and then draw your own conclusions.

With Von Mellenthin I had the following happen. He once said to me that I was moving around too much and breakfasting with the troops too often. I said "Come with me tomorrow and I'll show you something." We went forward, had a meeting with some front line officers, asked our questions about some relevant matters, and got some answers. So then I said to the officers "Let's go have lunch together." During lunch we asked the same questions and completely different facts came to light. I said to Mellenthin "You see why I go to eat with my people so often? Not because they cook so well, but because that's when I find out the truth."

In our last conversation you explained the concept of infantry, armor, artillery, and anti-armor, or PAK, as the four arms that comprised the German armored division. For Americans, the idea of organic anti-tank elements as a separate arm and force—not as a protective part of the infantry—suggests a new and intriguing solution to today's anti-tank problems. Who in the German Army first developed this concept and when?

Guderian developed the anti-tank idea at the same time that he was developing the idea of the tank. He had matured all these concepts well before 1929.

The Russians were also big in the use of anti-tank units. After all, we spent quite a while teaching them how. They had self-sufficient anti-tank brigades that they employed quite well—for instance, to strengthen the shoulders of a breakthrough in defense against German flank counterattacks.

You know, Guderian initially wanted to set up an all-armored army. His ideas were too modern to be well received but he fought like crazy for his ideas. He no sooner saw a superior than he already had him gored and was busy shaking him. It's interesting that without his very attractive and very competent wife he would never have succeeded. I always used to say that we would have won the war if Guderian had been permitted to bring his wife along.

In our conversations, we have discussed a number of the ideas fundamental to the German military approach, ideas such as the use of the schwerpunkt as a means of successively decentralizing control from army to platoon, and the critically important tradition of encouraging junior officers to criticize bluntly without fear of reprisal. Is there any important principle you would like to add to the various ones we have already discussed?

First and foremost, never follow a rigid scheme. Every situation is different—no two are the same. Even if they appear to be the same, in one case the troops will be fresh while in another they'll be fatigued. That difference will lead to completely different decisions.

I'm against the school approach that says, "In accordance with the ideas of the General Staff, in this situation you must do thus and such." On the contrary, you must proceed as dictated by the personalities involved and the particulars of the situation. For instance, you are attacking at seven o'clock in the morning and you have given clear tasks to each of your divisions: this one takes this objective, the next one grabs this, the third one does nothing except to protect the left flank. At the next attack opportunity you may have an almost identical situation, but everything must be changed completely because your most competent division commander has been killed in the meanwhile.

Therefore, one of the first principles has to be: There can be no fixed schemes. Every scheme, every pattern is wrong. No two situations are identical. That is why the study of military history can be extremely dangerous.

Another principle that follows from this is: Never do the same thing twice. Even if something works well for you once, by the second time the enemy will have adapted. So you have to think up something new.

No one thinks of becoming a great painter simply by imitating Michaelangelo. Similarly, you can't become a great military leader just by imitating so-and-so. It has to come from within. In the last analysis, military command is an art: one man can do it and most will never learn. After all, the world is not full of Raphaels either.

Lightning Source UK Ltd.
Milton Keynes UK
UKOW04f1829290415

250602UK00001B/43/P